The Sojourner's Road Home

Praise for *The Sojourner's Road Home: A 40-Day Journey to the Heart of God*

Our everyday life often seems insignificant when, actually, everyday life is our spiritual journey where choices and perspectives matter most. In *The Sojourner's Road Home*, author Kelly Mack McCoy delivers divine insight into the importance of the journey itself. Open these pages, and you will find the path to a closer walk with God.

~**Lana McAra,** best-selling, Christy Award-winning author
of forty-plus books

The Sojourner's Road Home causes us to reflect upon the spiritual battle raging all around us—a battle for our mind. The reason for this vicious and intense battle is that our minds are our greatest asset. When the things of the world cloud our minds, it becomes easy for us to feel lost and lose focus. We are unable to hear God, and so our sojourn here is without direction. We lose sight of what it is to have a personal relationship with Jesus Christ and struggle to find a way back to Him. *The Sojourner's Road Home* will help you find your way back. When we trust in God, we are not aimlessly wandering through life. He has a plan for each of us. This world is not our home. Heaven is our home. Our journey leads us home to God.

~**Ron Fraser,** M.Div., BCPCC, president and CEO of TFC Global,
and co-author of *A Chaplain's Heart*

The Sojourner's Road Home reinforces the true meaning in life that comes through a personal relationship with Jesus Christ. Readers (sojourners) are challenged to reflect upon each aspect of that relationship by measuring where they are in relation to what God has for them.

~**Dr. Morris Isara,** author of *What Now, God?*
and founder of Shepherds Wellspring Ministries

The Sojourner's Road Home is a superb devotional for travelers in the journey of life. Each day's insights are shared in a down-to-earth tone mixed with thought-provoking questions and quick wit. You'll find the stories relatable and interesting and the praise and prayer prompts on-target. Kelly Mack McCoy has written a 40-day roadmap to Home—a roadmap I can see myself perusing many times over.

~**Brenda Blanchard,** editor, author of *No Greater Love: 40 Prayers of Preparation and Praise*, and *Light in the Darkness* (release date Fall 2023)

The Sojourners Road Home is a great devotional to take with you wherever your journey leads you. The road we travel through this life can often become lonely and challenging when we miss the fellowship of others. But God the Holy Spirit is always present in our lives. He is our true traveling partner guiding our lives on the road home. As we travel the road of faith, we are assured we are not traveling alone. This forty-day journey to the heart of God reminds us of this truth and is an excellent resource for our life of faith.

~**Timothy Jones,** pastor, missionary, certified coach, speaker, and trainer. Founder of Go to the Truth Ministries

The Sojourner's Road Home is an excellent resource for anyone new to the Christian faith who is struggling to figure out what the next steps in this journey are. Kelly Mack McCoy does an excellent job of laying out Biblical truth in a line-upon-line and precept-upon-precept manner. Even as an older Christian, I found much-needed reminders of truth that have given the importance of my faith a fresh perspective. *The Sojourner's Road Home* will help solidify your faith and give you practical truths that can be put into practice daily. This is an easy-to-understand breakdown of the Christian life that is simple enough for a child to learn from, yet deep enough that the most experienced Christian should read it to gain an understanding of why we do what we do. If you have not read *The Sojourner's Road Home,* what are you waiting for?

~**Josh Rarrick,** founder of IMPACT (Independent Missionary Pilots Association) Ministries 360

We all have stories to tell about our sojourn in this broken, dysfunctional world. We can choose to become a victim of the dysfunction, or we can be a victor. *The Sojourner's Road Home* will help you find your way to the narrow road back Home and discover your journey's purpose. Before you read the book, a spoiler alert: God wants you to be a victor! We met Kelly Mack McCoy divinely through mutual connections when we chose to leave our 'normal' lives behind and follow The Radical Road God had for us. One of the reasons for that divine encounter is that the author is also a ghostwriter who is writing our story for us in our upcoming book.

~**Matt and Jess Pealer,** The Radical Road Podcast,
authors of *Life is Never a Straight Line*

An encouraging Bible devotional is like a good home-cooked meal for the soul. Kelly Mack McCoy serves weary travelers with nourishing and tasty meals in *The Sojourner's Road Home.*

~**Phillip Telfer,** pastor, author, director of Media Talk 101,
and founder of the Christian Worldview Film Festival

In *The Sojourner's Road Home,* Kelly Mack McCoy redirects our focus to our journey's road map—the Bible—and our internal GPS, The Holy Spirit, to keep us on the right path. His use of thought-provoking quotes and examples found in Scripture encourages us to continue the journey to the heart of God. That encouragement is found in every well-written day of the journey.

~**Ron Smith,** director of Business Development,
Neighborhood Bridges

I truly believe that God speaks through us in so many ways. Using the words of Scripture, Kelly Mack McCoy writes simply yet profoundly and moves our hearts to listen to God's voice and to trust in His word. Now is the time that God is calling on His people to come together in faith, and this beautiful heartfelt devotional is a great tool for daily reflection and worship.

~**Tracy Slepcevic,** best-selling author of *Warrior Mom,* speaker,
and integrative health coach

Kelly Mack McCoy has written an inspiring and transformational book about our journey to the heart of God. His easy-to-read style encourages and challenges us to stay on the narrow road, whether we are just beginning our spiritual journey or have walked with God for many years. Each day's reflection offers insight into how we can better understand God's love and grace and how it impacts our incredible sojourn here. The Sojourners Road Home redirects us away from the eight-lane, noisy, chaotic Interstate to the narrow, quiet, scenic road God designed. Walking the almost 8-foot-wide path, much like the one I traveled on as a boy will enable us to breathe deeply and discern all of the biblical riches He has for each of us.

~**Dr. John W. Lovitt**, LPC-S, president & CEO of The Family Wellness Institute and author of *Who's Listening Anyway?*

The Sojourner's Road Home is a book you'll pick up every morning to read and then record your praises and prayers on each day of your journey. Travelers come from many different backgrounds, but we have one thing in common—the road we travel can be lonely. *The Sojourner's Road Home* is like having a loving friend to travel with you on your journey.

~**Jim Houchens,** Traveling Mercies RV Ministry

The Sojourner's Road Home isn't just a forty-day journal. It could—*should*—be used every forty-day span for the rest of our lives. With its poignant stories, historical content, and scriptural references, readers (sojourners) will find wisdom every time they finish the last day and then re-open it to the first.

~**Cortney Donelson**, award-winning author of several faith-based books, including *Clay Jar, Cracked: When We're Broken But Not Shattered,* and owner of vocem LLC

THE
SOJOURNER'S
Road Home

A 40-DAY JOURNEY TO THE HEART OF GOD

KELLY MACK MCCOY

NASHVILLE

NEW YORK • LONDON • MELBOURNE • VANCOUVER

The Sojourner's Road Home

A 40-Day Journey to the Heart of God

Published in New York, New York, by Morgan James Publishing. Morgan James is a trademark of Morgan James, LLC. www.MorganJamesPublishing.com

Proudly distributed by Publishers Group West®

Scripture taken from the New King James Version®. Copyright © 1982 by Thomas Nelson. Used by permission. All rights reserved.

Morgan James BOGO™

A **FREE** ebook edition is available for you or a friend with the purchase of this print book.

CLEARLY SIGN YOUR NAME ABOVE

Instructions to claim your free ebook edition:
1. Visit MorganJamesBOGO.com
2. Sign your name CLEARLY in the space above
3. Complete the form and submit a photo of this entire page
4. You or your friend can download the ebook to your preferred device

ISBN 9781636981093 paperback
ISBN 9781636981109 ebook
Library of Congress Control Number:
2022950131

Cover Design by:
Rachel Lopez
www.r2cdesign.com

Interior Design by:
Christopher Kirk
www.GFSstudio.com

Morgan James is a proud partner of Habitat for Humanity Peninsula and Greater Williamsburg. Partners in building since 2006.

Get involved today! Visit: www.morgan-james-publishing.com/giving-back

To the sojourners who have trod the narrow road before us
and left a solid path to follow.
(Psalm 39:12)

TABLE OF CONTENTS

ACKNOWLEDGMENTS

Day 20, right in the middle of the forty-day journey, talks about detours or side trips we'll take during our sojourn here. As happened to most readers of this book, my life's journey took a detour when the whole world turned upside-down during recent events that caused much suffering and widespread despair.

First, I thank God for providing me with the inspiration, vision, and motivation to take on this project in the midst of a devastating time for many. I reminded myself that I'm just passing through this world and knew many of my fellow sojourners were in need of that reminder as well. I had another book planned, but my internal GPS, the Holy Spirit, told me it was time to recalculate.

To my family members who have given me much love and support during my sojourn through this broken world. To my wife, Emily, who took care of so many things that escaped my notice while I worked on this project, I am forever grateful. To my daughters, Brittni, Briana, and Kelly Jean, you have shown me so much about how love matters more than anything to be gained in this life and provided me with grandchildren to boot! To my son Patrick, your sojourn was cut short, but you impacted many lives during your brief time here on earth. We'll have an eternity to work on those projects together on the other side my dear son.

To my editor, Brenda Blanchard, who encouraged me in my writing journey from the beginning and taught me many things about the perplexities of the English language that sometimes push writers over the edge. You burned the midnight oil to get my manuscript back before the deadline only to have me revisit the manuscript once more to make changes and additions.

To the team at Morgan James Publishing. You have all inspired me from the beginning of our relationship. To David Hancock, who saw my vision for *The Sojourner's Road Home* from the time he received an early version of the manuscript in the proposal sent to Morgan James. Team members Emily Madison and Jim Howard helped develop the expanded vision for the manuscript into the book you hold in your hands. And to my fellow Morgan James author, and Warrior Mom, Tracy Slepcevic, who helped with the final edits. Thank you.

The Morgan James design team took the vision and developed the cover, and interior design that makes the book so much more appealing to readers, much like a chef at a five-star restaurant transforms ingredients to make the dining experience memorable.

FOREWORD

When I looked across the shore of the river where my grandparents lived and saw the seaplane docked there, I knew my life would be spent traveling the skyways. My father died when I was just two years of age. My grandparents encouraged my newfound love of airplanes from the moment I came to live with them.

My dream of becoming a pilot became a reality while still in my teens. As one of Canada's youngest licensed pilots at nineteen years of age, I flew into remote areas accessible only by air for much of the year.

I later became a captain for a major airline, where I spent my time traveling from Toronto to Timbuktu and everywhere in between, enjoying the highlife as I went. A dream life, right? If I wanted anything, I bought it. If I wanted to travel anywhere, I went. Just about all the world had to offer was at my fingertips.

But my high-flying dream life came crashing down to earth, metaphorically speaking, when I contracted a rare debilitating condition that left me unable to live any kind of normal life, much less fly a plane. I became no less of an addict than a junkie on skid row when I overmedicated myself to relieve the excruciating pain I felt every waking moment. I wanted to die.

And die, I did. When my life ended, I knew after a time that the body slumped over the wheel of my pickup in a remote area of Canada was mine. But I looked on from the outside before being taken to my journey's end.

I met my Savior, who loved me through it all as well as the deceivers who sought to pull me away from Him.

Eleven hours passed as the world measured time before I re-entered my brain-dead body. My body was not in my pickup in the remote area I left it but was in a hospital bed where it, much to the amazement of the medical staff, became alive once more.

I didn't know why I was carried away, but I knew I didn't want to return. The Lord chose that experience for me, and He chose to send me back. Since that time, I've dedicated my life to sharing the story of God's mercy and love and telling others about the new life which is available to all who seek Him.

Kelly Mack McCoy has traveled a much different road than mine through this life, but we are both sojourners here, as are you. In *The Sojourners Road Home, A 40-Day Journey to the Heart of God*, the author extends a hand to his fellow battered and bruised sojourners as an invitation to accompany him on the road to his or her own spiritual journey home.

Having spent the better part of his life traveling through this broken world alone, away from family, friends, and fellowship, Kelly Mack McCoy knows well the often-lonely path of a sojourner seeking to find his way back home. He wrote this devotional in response to events that have driven many to despair.

If our hope were in the world, there would indeed be a reason for despair. But as you take the forty-day journey, you will become less concerned with today's headlines and the struggles in your life when your focus turns to the heart of God. Each day you will read a brief devotion and story about the sojourner's life and then jot down your personal praises and prayers for the day.

As an airline pilot, I had the privilege of traveling the globe and experiencing all the world had to offer. But every runway ended in the same empty field of broken dreams. There is nothing like coming home and having a sense of place. That place isn't *in* or *of* the world. It is *in* the heart of the God who is love and who waits to receive you with open arms.

When I heard about Kelly Mack McCoy's book, *The Sojourner's Road Home, A 40-Day Journey to the Heart of God*, I knew it was something I wanted to read. It is no accident that you picked up this book any more than it was an accident that I was brain-dead for those eleven hours before coming back to this life to encourage you on your own sojourn through this foreign land.

Take the forty-day journey, my friend and fellow sojourner. We will journey together toward those open arms of the Savior who welcomed me to the eternal home He has provided for me—and you if you choose to come home to Him.

-Jim Woodford, author of *Heaven, An Unexpected Journey*

PREFACE

Our sojourn takes us through a troubled land in tumultuous times, but we can find comfort in knowing we are not aimlessly wandering on the road of life. The journey grows in meaning when we realize we're heading home to the welcoming embrace of our loving Father in heaven. We can now turn our focus away from the troubles on our road and towards a heart-throbbing expectancy because we know we're heading straight for that embrace, regardless of how many times we may stumble and fall along the way.

Recent events have left many feeling depressed and isolated. Good, hard-working people have lost their livelihoods and homes. Drug and alcohol abuse rates have skyrocketed. Incidents of family and civil strife are on the rise. Sadly, more people than ever are living in a state of fear of the future, a.k.a., Anticipatory Anxiety.

We need hope and a sense of community. One role of the church is to provide a sense of community in the best of times and in the worst of times. That need is greatest in times of crisis. But many churches closed their doors during these times of crisis and discouraged physical contact, leaving members feeling isolated and alone. The message repeated time and again is to keep our distance from others. Engagement with a church community is challenging, especially for those of us who spend much of our time on the road.

But there is some great news! God is there with us whenever we're isolated from others or in a crowd of strangers. We may experience the sense of belonging found in the Christian experience even while separated from others.

Scripture is filled with stories encouraging us to press on when we feel alone and isolated. Jesus Himself is the best example of this. He spent forty days alone in the desert except for the presence of the devil who tempted Him.

How about the Apostle Paul? He spent years in prison or under house arrest. And Joseph? His time in prison was even worse. He was thrown down into a dark, dank hole of a prison, where he remained for years, seemingly forgotten. The 20/20 benefit of biblical hindsight allows us to see how God worked in their lives and how their struggles related to His larger plan.

But these are great men of old. Powerful, towering, larger-than-life characters. What about you and me? Like the sojourners of old, we won't understand the purpose of many of our painful experiences until we make it home at our journey's end. But you can know this one thing for sure; He is working in your life right now as you read this.

The collection of devotions in this book is designed for those of us who travel or spend much of our time separated from others. The Bible recounts many more stories about the sojourners of old who experienced various trials in their travels. They overcame, and so shall we.

On each day of your journey through this devotional, you will read a brief story about a biblical or historical figure and even a few about everyday people like you and me. You can lay hold of your faith in a new and vibrant manner as you overcome feelings of fear arising from isolation and loneliness.

A forty-day period preceded some amazing breakthroughs in scripture. Jesus fasted for forty days before facing—and overcoming—the greatest temptation anyone has ever experienced. And He walked with His disciples and blessed them before ascending to Heaven forty days after His resurrection.

The Scripture references and stories in these devotions are designed to help us reflect on our circumstances on the road of life and how they relate to God's plan for us. *The Sojourner's Road Home: A 40-Day Journey to the Heart of God* is just the beginning of the journey of a lifetime.

May your Anticipatory Anxiety be replaced with Anticipatory Joy. Psychologists tell us that when we anticipate good things in the future, we'll work toward goals that will bring the desired outcome. When you belong to Christ, your GPS is set for your eternal destination with God in Heaven. He has placed Eternity in your heart so you may press on through the rest of your time here with joy (Philippians 3:14).

Take the 40-Day Journey. Your sojourn here will never be the same.

INTRODUCTION

I will not allow my life's light to be determined by the darkness around me.
~Sojourner Truth

And Jacob said to Pharaoh, "The days of the years of my pilgrimage
are one hundred and thirty years; few and evil have been the days
of the years of my life, and they have not attained to the days of the
years of the life of my fathers in the days of their pilgrimage."
(Genesis 47:9)

God designed us to have fellowship with one another to share our burdens. But when much of our time is spent away from home, we often feel isolated from our community and sometimes even from God. Are you in a line of work that requires you to spend a significant amount of time traveling; or perhaps isolated from others for another reason? Many are disengaged from society because of long-term illness, transportation issues, community violence, disabilities, anxiety, depression, etc. If you are in any of these situations, this book will be especially relevant for you.

Each day of our journey through life takes us from sunup to sundown; each week from one Sabbath to another. The seasons bring changes for which we must prepare. A new year dawns, and we will often find ourselves in a much different place than where we were at the beginning of the last. Life is a journey of journeys, a pilgrimage in a foreign land.

As Christians, we are citizens of the kingdom of Heaven (Philippians 3:20). We are not wandering aimlessly through this world. Heaven is our home. Our journey leads home to God, and we are moving closer to our destination with each passing day. He lives in us and will always be with us during our sojourn. Jesus Himself said, ". . . I am with you always, even to the end of the age" (Matthew 28:20).

God alone knows how long our journey on this earth will be. The highway of life presents us with many challenges in our journey through this alien land, however long we are here.

We have little choice about many things we face during our journey here. Our sojourn through this world is made with the body (vehicle) God has provided for us (Isaiah 64:8). And we often have little control over the obstacles we encounter. The good news is that the narrow road we travel leads to home regardless of our challenges.

But we can make our journey more difficult than it might otherwise be by the decisions we make along the way. Will we remember that God is with us as we travel, or will we try to go it alone? Will we listen to Him and journey according to His plans for us, or will we ignore Him and do our own thing?

There is a roadmap He provides for us—the Bible. And an internal GPS, the Holy Spirit. But will we follow that roadmap and listen to the GPS, or try to find our way there on our own? Will we make enough fuel stops to be sure we have good fuel for the journey and perform proper maintenance on our vehicle? Or will we drive ourselves until we're like an old clunker on fumes hoping to get there before the wheels fall off?

The Sojourner's Road Home: A 40-Day Journey to the Heart of God has a scripture passage and brief devotional with *your journey* as the theme for each of the 40 days. A praise and prayer prompt follows each devotion so you may be encouraged to begin each day with praise and thanksgiving to God, followed by prayer. Space is provided on the page opposite the day's devotional so that you may refer to it while writing down your words of praise and prayer.

Many studies have shown the importance of writing down the things we wish to remember and implement into our lives. Most of the thoughts I selected at the top of each day's devotions were expressions I found worthy to ponder and had recorded in my own journals. Several books have been written about the concept of journaling.

According to Merriam-Webster, a journal is a record of experiences, ideas, or reflections. Or as a verb, to record daily thoughts, experiences, etc. The English word journal originates from an Old French word, jour, as in soup du jour or, soup of the day. Journey originates from Journee, meaning a day's travel or work. You'll be recording your thoughts each day of your travel through this foreign land during your brief sojourn here.

Our journey has a definite destination when we give our lives to Christ. And our GPS is set for that destination. When we venture off course, as we all do from time to time, a new route is provided for us. But the destination never changes. We are en route to the embrace of our loving Father, who is waiting to receive us with open arms.

When you reach the end of the narrow road at the close of your journey through this world, your troubles will pass like signposts in the night. It will all be worth it when you hear Him say:

"Well done, good and faithful servant;
you have been faithful over a few things,
I will make you ruler over many things.
Enter into the joy of your lord."
(Matthew 25:23)

DAY 1

Not of This World

My home is in Heaven. I'm just traveling through this world.
~Billy Graham

Jesus answered, "My kingdom is not of this world. If My kingdom were of this world, My servants would fight, so that I should not be delivered to the Jews; but now My kingdom is not from here."
(John 18:36)

Jesus Christ was a sojourner on this earth. He was a King from another country. Why would this King leave His glorious kingdom to be born into a poor family and live as a common laborer only to die a horrible death on the cross? Why did He choose such a life for His journey here? He must have had a greater purpose than that.

God does not do random things. He sent His Son to live and die and then live again when He overcame death and the grave so that *we* might live! Jesus came for you and me. He came so our true home could be with Him in *His* country. He came so that *He* could be our true home.

Have you put your faith in Him? Have you accepted Jesus as Lord and made *His* home *your* home? If you have, He has prepared a place for *you* in His Father's house in Heaven (John 14:2). You now dwell in your spiritual home with God as you travel the road back to Him into the eternal dwelling place.

Jesus was just passing through this world as He traveled from Eternity to Eternity. His sojourn here ended on the cross before He was raised in glory. How will your sojourn end? Will you be raised with Him? If you choose to believe in Jesus as Lord, He's coming back for *you*.

May your sojourn in this world have meaning and purpose from this day forward.

Praise the Lord for bearing your sins on the cross of Calvary and giving you eternal life. Pray for His help and guidance during your sojourn through this foreign land as you journey home.

DAY 2

Buried and Raised

Baptism is faith in action.
~ Watchman Nee

And behold, a certain disciple was there, named Timothy, the son
of a certain Jewish woman who believed, but his father was Greek.
He was well spoken of by the brethren who were at Lystra and
Iconium. Paul wanted to have him go on with him. And he took him
and circumcised him because of the Jews who were in that region,
for they all knew that his father was Greek.
(Acts 16:1–3)

Timothy was considered Jewish because his mother was a Jew. His father
was Greek, however, so Timothy had not been circumcised as was required of
all Jews. But he willingly allowed himself to be circumcised as a young man
for the sake of the Jews that Paul (and now Timothy) were trying to reach.

Imagine yourself in Timothy's sandals. He is invited along on a journey
with Paul. What an incredible opportunity for a young man like him! A fantastic adventure lay ahead for him. But there was a cost. A very steep price
indeed. He had to make a serious commitment before he was allowed to take
the journey of a lifetime.

And some of us have trouble publicly identifying with Christ through
baptism? Salvation and baptism are the first two steps we take to start a new
life in our sojourn in this world. We are buried with Christ and then raised
in the newness of life.

Have you been baptized since you believed? Are you ready to publicly
commit to Christ throughout the rest of your sojourn here? Be raised in the
newness of life with Him.

Praise the Lord for dying on the cross, so you may be saved.
Ask the Lord to give you boldness in sharing your testimony
of how you came to believe in Jesus as Lord. If you haven't been
baptized, seek out a local church and speak to the pastor
about being baptized.

DAY 3

Our Journey with the Good Shepherd

*It takes some of us a lifetime to learn that Christ, our Good Shepherd,
knows exactly what He is doing with us. He understands us perfectly.*
~ *W. Phillip Keller*

". . .Your rod and Your staff, they comfort me...
You anoint my head with oil . . ."
(Psalm 23:4–5)

Like the sheep of His pasture, we journey through life under the care of our Good Shepherd. Does your life sometimes seem out of control? Psalm 23 makes sense of it all and comforts us with the image of His rod and staff as well as His anointing.

The rod of the shepherd in ancient times was primarily used to protect sheep from wolves and other predators who prowled around, seeking to devour them. But it could also be used for discipline to correct the sheep when they wandered off into danger.

The staff of our Shepherd guides us and keeps us in the flock. The hook of the staff was used as a guide to help keep wandering sheep on the right path. We are never alone. His rod and His staff bring comfort to us. He provides both guidance and discipline during our sojourn here.

But what about the anointing? We think of anointing as a ceremonial act setting aside a person for God's purpose, and it is. Why were the sheep anointed with oil? That anointing was done primarily to protect them from disease and torment caused by parasites like flies and mites—but also to protect the sheep from themselves.

Sheep will spread parasites among the flock by playful head-butting and rubbing. Also, the rams may cause injury to themselves and others when they butt heads. The oil causes the blows to brush off harmlessly to the side, much to the chagrin of the males of the flock.

Praise the Lord for being the Good Shepherd He is. Pray that you will yield to His guidance and discipline as you journey through a multitude of perilous paths in this world.

DAY 4

Traveling Companion

What a friend we have in Jesus
All our sins and griefs to bear…
~Poem turned hymn by Joseph M. Scriven

"A friend loves at all times, And a brother is born for adversity."
(Proverbs 17:17)

Books and papers scattered across the hallway as Jonathan hit the floor. As he picked up his glasses to better see the bully who tripped him, he braced himself for the humiliation he knew would follow. There was always more humiliation. Jonathan had long been a target of bullies at his school. The bully pushed Jonathan's head down as he walked away.

"Hey, I saw you trip him." All eyes turned to Mark. Jonathan's fellow student Mark was one of the friendliest kids in the school. He also had a reputation for being one of the toughest. Mark grasped the bully's shirt, and asked, "How would you like me to trip you?"

Mark and Jonathan attended the same church. This incident began a friendship that would last into old age. The bully? He promised never to touch Jonathan again.

Do you have companions who travel with you on your journey? If so, you are blessed beyond measure. Seventeenth-century English preacher Thomas Fuller said, "If you have one true friend, you have more than your share."

You may not think you have such a friendship. But you have something far more precious. You have a friendship with Jesus that will last an eternity. He is your traveling companion forever.

*Praise the Lord for being your friend and traveling companion
even when you feel alone. Pray He will bring people into your life
who need the friendship you can provide.*

DAY 5

Citizens of Heaven

Traveling with God in a "no frills" way results in a life that is missing out on the blessings and abundance of God. You still arrive at your destination, but it's far less enjoyable than it could be.
~ Barry Voss

Beloved, I beg you as sojourners and pilgrims, abstain
from fleshly lusts which war against the soul, having your conduct
honorable among the Gentiles, that when they speak
against you as evildoers, they may, by your good works
which they observe, glorify God in the day of visitation.
(1 Peter 2:11–12)

Do those we interact with during our travels know they're dealing with citizens of Heaven? Is there something about us that says we're different? Do we show genuine love for others? Is our integrity and character evident to all?

When we meet others during our travels, our conduct should cause them to 'glorify God in the day of visitation?' Many times, we represent our company or business during this earthly sojourn. We are, in a sense, ambassadors. How we define our business will often determine whether people we encounter will want to have a relationship with our company.

In the spiritual realm, we represent the Christ who redeemed our very souls (Psalm 49:15). As we travel the road of life, shouldn't we be concerned about whether others will want to have a relationship with Him based on what they see in us? We are now *His* ambassadors (2 Corinthians 5:20).

To keep our 'conduct honorable among the [world],' considering all the temptations and challenges we face, we must ask God to give us the strength to do so *daily*. Let's meditate on The Lord's Prayer (Matthew 6:9–13) often during our sojourn here.

Praise the Lord for making you a citizen of Heaven. Pray that He will transform you into His image so others who seek to become citizens of His heavenly Kingdom will be drawn to you.

DAY 6

Longing for Home

My hope is built on nothing less Than Jesus Christ, my righteousness.
~From a hymn by Edward Mote

For we are aliens and pilgrims before You,
As were all our fathers;
Our days on earth are as a shadow,
And without hope.
(1 Chronicles 29:15)

King David dedicated the offering of the Israelites to the temple. But his son, Solomon, would be the one to build it for the worship of the Lord. The people had given generously and joyfully at the dedication. David said in the verse before the one above that everything they had belonged to God and everything they could give Him was already His.

The Israelites were living in the promised land given to them by God. And yet they knew they were only travelers or sojourners in this world. Some versions of 1 Chronicles 29:15 use the word sojourners when describing God's people. All of them convey the meaning of temporary residents just passing through. After living in slavery in Egypt for over 400 years before wandering the desert for yet another forty years, the Israelites were in the home promised to them. Still, they knew it was but a temporary dwelling place.

We may become weary and feel hopeless when we are on the road for days or weeks. We may become homesick and long to return to a familiar place. Should we not then long even more for our God, seek to know Him, and yearn to be with Him in our eternal home in Heaven? When we belong to God, we are not without hope; we are hope-filled.

Praise the Lord for the hope He placed in your heart when you came to know Him. Pray He will use you in your sojourn here so your fellow travelers will come to know Him and become hope-filled as well.

THE
SOJOURNER'S
Road Home

KEEP RIGHT

FOLLOW THE NARROW ROAD

DAY 7

Excess Baggage

Resentment is like drinking poison
and waiting for the other person to die.
~Augustine of Hippo

Brethren, I do not count myself to have apprehended; but one thing I
do, forgetting those things which are behind and reaching forward
to those things which are ahead, I press toward the goal for the prize
of the upward call of God in Christ Jesus.
(Philippians 3:13–14)

Our rearview mirror has a purpose. We can see where we've been and view possible dangers coming from behind us. In a spiritual sense, when we're honest about our past, we can turn from our sins and avoid repeating our mistakes.

But how often do we allow our past to haunt us instead? Are we carrying excess baggage from our past that hinders our journey ahead? Why drag that extra weight around with us? Isn't it far better to look ahead than behind during our journey through this life? After all, when driving along our road here, we spend most of our time focusing on what's ahead of us while glancing in the mirror to see where we've been.

If we feel we can't move forward because of something that happened in our past, we are carrying heavy baggage that needs to be left behind. The heaviest load we may carry is the burden of unforgiveness. It is God's job to deal with people who may have hurt us in the past. Let's get out of the way and let Him do His work in them. Only then will we be able to let go of the hurt and begin ". . . reaching forward to those things which are ahead . . ."

Praise the Lord for forgiving your sin and lifting the heavy burden of guilt from you. Pray He will reveal to you the unnecessary baggage you are carrying around that hinders your journey and give you the heart to forgive others.

THE
SOJOURNER'S
Road Home

DAY 8

Love for Hate

*Returning hate for hate multiplies hate, adding deeper darkness to a
night already devoid of stars. Darkness cannot drive out darkness; only
light can do that. Hate cannot drive out hate; only love can do that.*
~Martin Luther King Jr.

And when His disciples James and John saw this, they said,
"Lord, do You want us to command fire to come down from heaven
and consume them, just as Elijah did?" But He turned and rebuked
them, and said, "You do not know what manner of spirit you are of.
For the Son of Man did not come to destroy men's lives
but to save them." And they went to another village.
(Luke 9:54–56)

The Samaritans' prejudices toward Jews kept them from seeing the
Savior for who He was. But those prejudices against Him didn't keep Jesus
from seeing their need. The disciples, however, were of a particular 'manner
of spirit' when they suggested killing the Samaritans. They had much to
learn about the reasons behind their words and attitudes, as do we in the
times in which we live.

This same 'manner of spirit' often controls how we see others and deter-
mines how we treat them. Jesus came into this world to be a light in the
darkness, not to fight darkness with more darkness. We should follow His
example on our journey and save lives rather than destroy them.

He called us to love our enemies. But we often allow our prejudices
(and we all have them) to determine how we see others. Prejudice means
prejudgment. How often do we judge others *before* we even know the truth
about them?

Praise the Lord for being the loving Father He is even when you have withheld love for others. Pray He will purify your heart and give you unconditional love for others—especially when they are different from you and perhaps difficult to understand.

THE
SOJOURNER'S
Road Home

KEEP RIGHT

FOLLOW THE NARROW ROAD

DAY 9

Narrow Road Ahead

God's plan for moving people from the broad road
to the narrow road involves you.
~Alistair Begg

Enter by the narrow gate; for wide is the gate and broad is the way that
leads to destruction, and there are many who go in by it.
Because narrow is the gate and difficult is the way which leads to life,
and there are few who find it.
(Matthew 7:13–14)

Few people travel on narrow roads because they can't go as fast, and
those roads are much more challenging to navigate. It can also be dangerous
at times if that narrow road winds down the side of a mountain. And you
may miss a turn that can get you off course for a while. In contrast, the
Interstate Highway System roads are wide and straight where possible and
thus much easier to follow.

But Jesus warned against taking the wide, straight, and most popular
road. Driving the Interstate hopefully won't lead to your destruction, but
traveling the wide alternative to Christ's narrow way *will* lead to destruction.
Why then, are so many traveling the broad path? Because it's easier, faster,
and more comfortable. But that popular road doesn't go where we want to be.

It's the destination that matters. The Road to Hana on the island of
Maui in Hawaii, with its 617 turns and fifty-six one-lane bridges, can be seen
as a metaphor for the narrow road. Those turns can be scary, often leaving
you unable to see oncoming traffic. But you get to see the beauty of God's
creation when you stop at the bridges. Sometimes we may need to slow
down on our journey or stand still before Him and marvel at the beauty of
His creation. Those are times of refreshing for our souls when we spend time
with the Lord and listen for His direction.

Praise the Lord for guiding you to the narrow road.
Pray that He will use you as a guide to help those
on the road to destruction find the road to life.

DAY 10

Just Passing Through

If a man neglects the kingdom of God,
nothing which he can obtain is really valuable to him.
~ Charles Finney

Then God blessed them, and God said to them, "Be fruitful and multiply;
fill the earth and subdue it; have dominion over the fish of the sea, over
the birds of the air, and over every living thing that moves on the earth."
(Genesis 1:28)

God made man in his image (Genesis 1:26–27) and instructed them to
'fill the earth.' What a fantastic journey was ahead for them! Adam and Eve,
and their descendants who followed His command, could not have known
where their travels would take them.

But what was meant to be a beautiful journey eventually led to a dead
end. Why? Because they rebelled against their Creator. God caused a Great
Flood to cover the earth that drowned all of Adam's descendants. All except
the righteous Noah and his family, that is.

Noah built an ark at God's direction and to His specifications, so Noah
and his family lived. After the flood waters receded, Noah stepped out of that
ark and into a much different world than Adam had initially found himself
in over a thousand years earlier. But God repeated His instructions to Noah
and told him to 'fill the earth.'

It was only a few centuries after Noah left the ark that men decided to
stop in Babel to build a great tower to reach the heavens as a monument to
their imagined greatness (Genesis 11:4). But God put an end to their foolishness by confusing their language, which forced them to abandon their plan
and continue His. Their folly would have inevitably led to their destruction.

This world is not our permanent home, so we shouldn't be surprised
when it doesn't feel like it is. Keep going, fellow sojourner.

Praise the Lord for the road He has given you to travel today.
Pray that when you experience sorrow or loss, He will remind you
of your eternal home in Heaven with Him.

KEEP RIGHT

FOLLOW THE NARROW ROAD

DAY 11

Diverging Roads

Two roads diverged in a yellow wood,
And sorry I could not travel both
And be one traveler, long I stood
And looked down one as far as I could
To where it bent in the undergrowth;
Then took the other, as just as fair,
And having perhaps the better claim,
Because it was grassy
and wanted wear;
Though as for that the passing there
Had worn them really about the same,

And both that morning equally lay
In leaves no step had trodden black.
Oh, I kept the first for another day!
Yet knowing how way leads on to way,
I doubted if I should ever come back.
I shall be telling this with a sigh
Somewhere ages and ages hence:
Two roads diverged in a wood,
and I—
I took the one less traveled by,
And that has made all the difference.

~ Robert Frost

If any of you lacks wisdom, let him ask of God, who gives to all liberally
and without reproach, and it will be given to him.
(James 1:5)

In Robert Frost's best-known and most-loved poem, *The Road Not Taken*, two roads diverged before the traveler. The traveler (sojourner) stood and pondered the choice that lay before him. There were only two roads there. To continue his journey, he was forced to decide whether to travel one or the other. He chose the one less traveled. That, he said, made all the difference.

We all make choices during our sojourn here that shape our destiny. The same choice faced by the traveler in Frost's poem is before us today. When we look back, will we be happy with the road we chose to take, or will we lament the road not taken? How can we know we are choosing the right path?

Ask God for wisdom. The narrow road will be the one less traveled.

Praise the Lord for His never changing ways. Pray He will guide you down the narrow road all the days of your life, so that you will not be deceived when choosing which path to take.

KEEP RIGHT

FOLLOW THE NARROW ROAD

DAY 12

Journey of (The Wai Wai) Faith

If childlike dependence on God is the mark of a great soul,
then there are great souls hidden in all sorts of places
where the world sees only disability, decay, and despair.
~ Colleen Carroll Campbell

Praise Him with the sound of the trumpet;
Praise Him with the lute and harp.
(Psalm 150:3)

Colonel John "Blashers" Blashford-Snell descended the Blue Nile, navigated the Congo, and fought terrorists during his journey here. He also was engaged in countless humanitarian aid missions around the world.

His most challenging assignment? According to Blashford-Snell, his most difficult task was transporting a baby grand piano deep into the Amazon rainforest so the remote Wai Wai tribe could place it on their dirt-covered floor for use during church services. Their village was converted to Christ by American missionaries in the 1950s.

The adventurer's greatest challenge entailed carrying the piano by hand five miles through the rainforest without damaging it after flying the piano as close as possible to the Wai Wai's tribal home. He was likely motivated by the engineering challenge and spirit of adventure, but God's purpose for the trip provided the tribe with the joyful means to worship Him they asked for.

"We're a very musical people; I'm sure we can play it," said the tribe's priest, who had requested a grand piano. With simple child-like faith, the tribe asked for a grand piano, believing they would receive one despite the seemingly impossible circumstances. God used Blashford-Snell to deliver it right to their door. His eye is on His children even deep in the Amazon rainforest. Our greatest adventure during our sojourn here may lie ahead when we trust God to provide in miraculous ways. Just as the Wai Wai did.

Praise the Lord for all He provides for you every day. Pray He will give you childlike faith like the members of the Wai Wai tribe.

DAY 13

The Pilgrim's Pathway

The Hill though high, I covet to ascend,
The difficulty will not me offend;
For I perceive the way to life lies here.
~ Christian from The Pilgrim's Progress

. . . being confident of this very thing, that He who has begun a good
work in you will complete it until the day of Jesus Christ . . .
(Philippians 1:6)

John Bunyan (1628–1688) wrote *The Pilgrim's Progress* from prison. He
served time for holding religious services outside the auspices of the established state church in England. His persecution and time spent in prison
gave him a keen understanding of the temporary nature of life in this world.
He came to understand we are pilgrims here with a definite destination.
He also felt that, as believers, we must make progress while we travel to our
eternal home.

Bunyan's book is an allegory chronicling the life of Christian, who car-
ries a great burden on his back. Evangelist tells Christian to travel to a far
country to relieve the burden (his sin) and journey on the narrow path until
he reaches the Celestial City of God. He faced many temptations to depart
from the path, but Christian grew in strength and maturity during his travels. Christian stumbled and fell along the way, but he always got back up and
onto the narrow road, which he followed until his journey ended.

The Pilgrim's Progress was published in 1678 and was once the second
most popular book in print after the Bible. Christian's journey from the City
of Destruction to the Celestial City is as representative of the sojourner's
journey now as it was then.

Praise the Lord for His good work in your life. Pray you will stay on the path He has for you despite the challenges and temptations you may face during your journey.

DAY 14

Coming Home

Difficulties are just things to overcome, after all.
~Ernest Shackleton

And he arose and came to his father. But when he was still a great
way off, his father saw him and had compassion,
and ran and fell on his neck and kissed him.
(Luke 15:20)

Ernest Shackleton, a renowned explorer of the Antarctic, became most famous not for reaching his destination but for arriving safely back home with his crew. His ship was aptly named the Endurance.

Sir Raymond Priestly, addressing the British Science Association in 1956, said, "Scott for scientific method, Amundsen for speed and efficiency but when disaster strikes and all hope is gone, get down on your knees and pray for Shackleton." Shackleton has been studied and emulated by leadership experts since his exploits were first known.

Our ultimate destination is not somewhere far away but to a safe return home. We will have struggles and experience some major failures along the road back home. Salvation in Greek means just that. The story of the prodigal son in the Bible is a story of coming home. Our Father waits for our return with welcoming arms. And He will provide a place for us at His table forever. "Please come home," He says.

Praise the Lord for His love and compassion for you even while you were in sin and rebellion against Him. Pray He will help you focus on your home with Him instead of the challenges you face.

DAY 15

Support Your Fellow Sojourners

The gospel is only good news if it gets there in time.
~ Carl F.H. Henry

Now a certain woman named Lydia heard us. She was a seller of purple
from the city of Thyatira, who worshiped God. The Lord opened her heart
to heed the things spoken by Paul. And when she and her household
were baptized, she begged us, saying, "If you have judged me to be
faithful to the Lord, come to my house and stay." So she persuaded us.
(Acts 16:14–15)

Paul and his traveling companions had sailed for weeks before disembarking in Philippi. God would open many doors for the Apostle there.
How would you have liked to have been involved in that ministry? What a
privilege! What an adventure!

Lydia, a woman of some means, decided she was all in after hearing
Paul preach to a group of women at a riverside place of prayer. Already a
worshiper of God, she was so moved by the message of the Gospel that she
asked for a way to serve the Church in Macedonia. Lydia opened her home
and hosted the young, growing Philippian congregation. Paul moved on and
continued his ministry to the Gentiles elsewhere.

Some of us, like Paul, are called to travel and spread the Good News
as we go. And some, like Lydia, are called to support the ministry of others
through prayer, fasting, financial offerings, and in a myriad of other ways.

Whether we go or stay, our encouragement of others *is* our ministry. We
are all part of one body—the Body of Christ. Let's all do our part to keep His
Body functioning as it should.

Praise the Lord for giving you the incredible honor of being part of the Body of Christ. Pray He will show you your role in helping to spread the Gospel, whatever your current position may be.

KEEP RIGHT

FOLLOW THE NARROW ROAD

DAY 16

Hidden Curve Ahead

When all men fail me;
You remember and seek me;
It is Your will that I should know You
And turn to You.
Lord, I hear Your call and follow;
Help me.
~Dietrich Bonhoeffer, Letters and Papers from Prison

And Jesus said to him, "Foxes have holes and birds of the air have
nests, but the Son of Man has nowhere to lay His head."
(Matthew 8:20)

We follow the One who never settled down on this earth. Jesus set about doing His Father's business on His journey. If we are following Jesus, we must go where He is going. What does that mean for us in the here and now? When Jesus was on this earth in bodily form, He told His disciples where to go at times. But sometimes He didn't. The disciples had to learn to trust Him every step of the way. Of course, Jesus knows where He is going and always has a plan. But He doesn't always reveal His plans to us.

This is where walking by faith comes in. But you're afraid you'll make mistakes? Join the crowd. We all make mistakes during our walk with Him. His disciples often stumbled and fell along the way as they followed Him. So shall we. Bonhoeffer said that the biggest mistake we can make in life is to always be afraid of making mistakes. Jesus has not changed (Hebrews 13:8). Neither has human nature. He now guides us by the Holy Spirit, who lives in us. We should be prepared to follow Him wherever He leads.

Praise the Lord for coming down from His heavenly home to show by His example how to live your life for Him. Pray He will prepare your heart to follow Him wherever He may lead you.

DAY 17

Our Unpredictable Journey

Fear is a self-imposed prison that will keep you
rom becoming what God intends for you to be.
You must move against it with the weapons of faith and love.
~ Rick Warren

Then He arose and rebuked the wind, and said to the sea, "Peace, be still!" And the wind ceased and there was a great calm. But He said to them, "Why are you so fearful? How is it that you have no faith?"
(Mark 4:39–40)

Jesus and His disciples embarked on a short journey across the unpredictable Sea of Galilee. Weary from His work, the Lord chose to lay His head down on a pillow and take a nap in the stern. A sudden, furious storm came upon them. Many of the disciples were commercial fishermen accustomed to navigating in storms. But the men feared for their lives because this storm was so fierce. The able seaman among them, John, James, Peter, and Andrew, cried out to Jesus, "Teacher, do you not care that we are perishing?"

We may be skilled at what we do and think we can handle what lies ahead during our journey. But we all know how unpredictable life can be. Things can and often do change in an instant. We often face storms for which we may not be prepared. Is it not wise then to start our journey with Jesus in our boat (or car or truck or plane)?

Praise the Lord for being unchangeable and immovable in the face of the storms you may encounter during your journey.
Pray that your fear will be cast out just as light dispels darkness when you focus on Him amid the storm. (2 Timothy 1:7)

DAY 18

When Is Enough, Enough?

Most of us are poor travelers. We forget we must put up
with a great deal on the journey that would be intolerable at home.
You are not home yet. Travel Light!
~Dr. David Allen

". . . and do not have two tunics apiece."
(Luke 9:3)

When Jesus sent His disciples to preach, he told them one tunic was enough. While that obviously isn't a legalistic command for us to follow today, it illustrates well the principle of being content with enough and how we should travel light during our sojourn through this world.

We tend to get attached to all the wrong things and accumulate much more than we need. Our closets are full, but we wear just a few of the clothes in them more than a handful of times. Our kitchen cupboards are full of cups we sort through to get to the favorite ones we use most of the time. Our homes are full of things we rarely use.

We run out of room and then provide more income for the $40 billion storage industry to store the rest. What insanity! Dave Ramsey said, "We buy things we don't need with money we don't have to impress people we don't like." And then we pay storage rental fees when we run out of room that, over time, are more expensive than the value of the contents in those storage units.

The armchair psychiatrists among us can debate the reasons for our strange behavior, but one thing we know for sure; we aren't taking any of our stuff with us. And if we don't even need it now, why are we hanging on to it? Let's travel light on our journey.

Praise the Lord for supplying all your needs. Pray He will give you the wisdom to understand what you need for your travels here and what wants and desires may be hindering your journey.

KEEP RIGHT

FOLLOW THE NARROW ROAD

DAY 19

Watch Your Step

Do not plunge headlong by the road of mortals,
on which you see for many shipwreck has occurred.
Step between the nets with hesitant feet,
for by those nets the rest we see were caught up unawares.
~ Columbanus, Irish Missionary, 543–615 A.D.

And if you call on the Father, who without partiality judges according to each
one's work, conduct yourselves throughout the time of your stay here in fear;
knowing that you were not redeemed with corruptible things, like silver or gold,
from your aimless conduct received by tradition from your fathers, but with the
precious blood of Christ, as of a lamb without blemish and without spot.
(1 Peter 1:17–19)

Alone and separated from his unit for some time, a soldier was on the
run for his life. He estimated he was perhaps ten miles from the border. If
he remained in enemy-controlled territory, he was in grave danger. His path
was nothing more than a well-worn cattle route—not a road at all. A herd of
cattle had trudged through rain-drenched farmland, digging deep pits which
were now hardened by the sun.

Each step forward threatened to end his journey and, thus, his life if he
hurried too much and sprained an ankle or injured a knee. Those ten miles
seemed like a thousand since he knew he would be a sitting duck for the
enemy if he were hurt. He had to stay focused and aware of the danger along
his path, or he would never make it home.

How should we spend our time during our sojourn through this alien
land? Our journey here takes us through enemy territory and can be likened
to a soldier behind enemy lines. We are citizens of another land now because
of our redemption through the precious blood of Jesus. We should, therefore,
"conduct [our]selves . . . in fear" and turn from the "aimless conduct" of our
past and focus instead on God and His Kingdom for the rest of our journey.

Praise the Lord for His glorious Kingdom and for allowing you, through His mercy, to be a citizen there. Pray He will strengthen you and prepare you for battle as you journey behind enemy lines.

THE
SOJOURNER'S
Road Home

KEEP RIGHT

FOLLOW THE NARROW ROAD

DAY 20

Side Trips

*God can use detours to get you **to your destiny.***
~ Tony Evans

Now there was a famine in the land, and Abram went down to Egypt to
dwell there, for the famine was severe in the land.
(Genesis 12:10)

Abraham (Abram) had to take a side trip because of trouble brewing
in the land. He didn't have his best moments in Egypt. Abraham was
fearful the Egyptians would kill him and take his beautiful wife, Sarai.
Since that was customary at the time, it wasn't an unreasonable fear. But
Abraham was not acting in faith. He made Sarai pretend she was only his
sister (Genesis 12:11–13).

Don't you love the Bible? The stories contained therein show the good,
the bad, and the ugly side of the characters revealed within its pages. God
intervened when Abraham committed that boneheaded lack of trust. By His
grace, disaster was averted.

We've all had our failings on our little side trips when we veer off the
narrow road. I'm thankful mine aren't recorded in a place for all the world
to see. Of course, God knows and has those documented as well. But thank
God, my failings, like Abraham's, have been forgiven.

Our sojourn here may include many side trips. The question each time
is, did God send us to where we are or did we veer off the road because we
failed to keep our eyes on Him? Are we on one of these side trips now? Has
God placed us in our current position for His purpose, or have we once again
veered off the narrow road onto our own path? God can intervene just as He
did with Abraham, regardless of where we are or how we got there.

Praise the Lord for His steadfast love and unchanging nature.
Thank Him for your own boneheaded or misguided detours, for He can
use even these for your growth and His glory. Pray He will help
keep you on the road leading to your Eternal destination.

KEEP RIGHT

FOLLOW THE NARROW ROAD

DAY 21

Time to Recalculate?

Along life's journey, there will always be times
when you have to recalculate.
~Michael Wilson

Repent therefore and be converted, that your sins may be blotted out,
so that times of refreshing may come from the presence of the Lord.
(Acts 3:19)

"Recalculating . . ." You know what this means. It's your GPS device's way of saying, 'You are going the wrong way. You need to turn around and get back on course.' I laugh at my GPS at times because the female voice I have it set to sounds like she's a little irritated with me for straying from the course she has for me. Going in the wrong direction causes the device to continually update itself, constantly calculating the best route to the destination it's set for.

Our spiritual GPS is set in the direction of our new home when we place our trust in Christ. The Holy Spirit will recalculate our journey each time we start going off course. Scripture speaks of our part in the process when He begins to nudge us back in the right direction. It's called repentance. We turn from the wrong path we're on and get back on that narrow road.

I'll turn off my GPS when I'm tired of being scolded by her. But when we don't listen to the voice of the Holy Spirit, we prolong a part of our journey by going in the wrong direction. We know that road doesn't lead where we ultimately want to go.

Praise the Lord for His unchanging, loving nature. Pray you will hear His voice calling you back to the right path when you've veered off course.

DAY 22

A Change in Plans

What a shame it would be if we were waiting for God to say
something, while He's been waiting on us to do something.
~Bob Goff

But I will tarry in Ephesus until Pentecost. For a great and effective
door has opened to me, and there are many adversaries.
(1 Corinthians 16:8–9)

We may have a general idea of God's purpose for our life. We think we know something about our destination on this earth. Perhaps it is to build our ministry or complete our education to serve Him in a career. It could be to settle in a particular place so we may serve God in retirement.

Regardless of our long-term decisions, we must remember that we live in the present with God each step of the way. We know He is always in the present with us, but it's easy for us to forget He's now present in the future as well. Many adversaries will gather like buzzards waiting for the kill when we do the Lord's will, but we need not fear them because our future is in God's hands.

Paul knew the Lord opened a great and effective door in Ephesus because of the fierce opposition he faced. Sometimes that's all we need to know—that God is doing something—and we need to let Him keep doing it. We'll need to know when to tarry at times, so our ears must be listening to His voice. God will also let us know when it's time to move on.

Is it time to move or stay? Where is God going? Has He opened doors for you or closed them?

Praise the Creator God for who He is: a God of action!
Pray you will be open to move—or tarry as He leads.

KEEP RIGHT

FOLLOW THE NARROW ROAD

DAY 23

Going Nowhere?

Security is mostly a superstition. It does not exist in nature,
nor do the children of men as a whole experience it.
Avoiding danger is no safer in the long run than outright exposure.
Life is either a daring adventure or nothing.
~Helen Keller

And your sons shall be shepherds in the wilderness for forty years,
and bear the brunt of your infidelity until your carcasses
are consumed in the wilderness.
(Numbers 14:33)

Sometimes we feel like we've been stuck in one place for too long. In 1998, Karl Bushby took the first step in what was to be a 36,000-mile walking journey around the world. The former British paratrooper called his journey the Goliath Expedition. His trip was to be an eight-year journey.

But difficulties in obtaining visas and sponsorships to help him through various financial crises significantly extended the timeframe for his journey. Rugged terrain along his route, such as the Russian tundra, also slowed him down. The challenges he experienced in gaining access to some of the countries he planned to cross resulted in his spending months in one place, going nowhere. As of this writing, Bushby is still walking.

The Israelites were stuck in the wilderness for forty years because of their sin. Circumstances beyond our control may keep us stuck where we are, making it impossible to continue our journey. Or it may be our sin keeping us from moving forward.

A great adventure lies ahead for us. But sometimes, we must remove the obstacles before continuing our journey.

Praise the Lord for every step of your journey thus far. He can use all your experiences for His glory and to prepare you for the road ahead. Pray that the Lord will reveal whether your circumstances are a consequence of your sin or events beyond your control.

KEEP RIGHT

FOLLOW THE NARROW ROAD

DAY 24

Time to Move On?

The place God calls you to is the place
where your deep gladness and the world's deep hunger meet.
~Frederick Buechner

As for Saul, he made havoc on the church, entering every house, and
dragging off men and women, committing them to prison. Therefore
those who were scattered went everywhere preaching the word. Then
Philip went down to the city of Samaria and preached Christ to them.
(Acts 8:3–5)

A pharisee named Saul persecuted the Church in Jerusalem with religious zeal. Many of Jesus' disciples may have thought they were failing in
their mission. But the Church and the world were about to experience a
radical change because of this persecution.

The disciples were forced to flee. Did they fail? Hardly. They brought
the Gospel with them everywhere they went. Saul had a dramatic conversion
and became Paul. The Apostle then ministered to some of the souls those
scattered disciples preached to. What a turn of events!

When we experience difficulties trying to do the same things that
worked for us in the past, it may be time for us to move on. Our adversaries
often cause problems to sidetrack us, but God can turn those problems into
new opportunities.

The Lord may be calling us to move on to another place. Or perhaps He
has new things for us where we are. Hopefully, we have matured during our
travels and learned to better discern His work in our lives.

When we have confirmation from Him, our job is to crank it up and
go—and not look back!

Praise the Lord for every road He has had you travel thus far. Pray He will open a new route leading to a place matching the desires of your heart so you may fulfill His calling in your life. We know we are given the desires of our hearts when we are faithfully serving His purpose for us.

THE
SOJOURNER'S
Road Home

KEEP RIGHT

FOLLOW THE NARROW ROAD

DAY 25

Traveling on Solid Ground

On Christ, the solid Rock, I stand;
All other ground is sinking sand.
~ From a hymn by Edward Mote

Trust in the Lord with all your heart,
And lean not on your own understanding;
In all your ways acknowledge Him,
And He shall direct your paths.
(Proverbs 3:5–6)

The soldiers were uncertain how long they could remain on their current path, but they were sure of one thing—staying on that path provided their only hope of returning home. Even the stars couldn't help to guide them through the darkness. A thick cover of clouds hovered above the hard ground beneath their feet. Flashlights would attract enemy fire. But they carried something with them that kept hope alive: their training.

The solid ground on which they stood assured them they traveled the right path. The men moved slowly, intensely focused on the feedback from the earth beneath their boots. When that earth began to soften, they knew they must return to the solid ground. The soldiers finally reached their destination by continuing on the firm path until safely past enemy lines.

As we navigate the many perils we may face during our travels in this fallen world, our mission is to focus on the solid Rock until we arrive home. Our journey will sometimes be dark, but the narrow road we travel is built on solid ground.

Praise the Lord for being the solid Rock you can always depend on.
Pray He will guide you through this fallen world and keep you
on the solid ground of His Word until you return to Him
after you reach the end of your sojourn here.

THE
SOJOURNER'S
Road Home

KEEP RIGHT

FOLLOW THE NARROW ROAD

DAY 26

The High Way Home

It's time to begin righting the story of your life.
~David Jeremiah

"Set up signposts,
Make landmarks;
Set your heart toward the highway,
The way in which you went.
Turn back, O virgin of Israel,
Turn back to these your cities."
(Jeremiah 31:21)

Returning home is a recurring theme in literature and movies. These stories often tell of a troubled protagonist who leaves home to escape from his past or find his way, thinking there are better roads and greener pastures for him over the horizon. Sometimes the protagonist is forced to leave because of rebellious behavior. Inward transformation happens when adventures out in the real world teach him lessons he refused to learn at home. He returns home as a changed and grateful person.

The nation of Israel had been exiled from the land God gave them because of their sin and rebellion against Him. God disciplined them while they were in exile. But He was now ready to bless them once more. And what must they do? Turn. They were to turn around and set their heart toward the highway home.

What are the markers and signposts? We follow markers and signposts when we're on the physical highways we travel here so we may know we're on the road taking us to where we want to go. Have you ever traveled down the highway in the wrong direction? All you can see are the backs of the road signs. You don't know where you're going. But you do know you're going the wrong way. The signs are as real and often as easy to see in our spiritual journey. We can't see them if we're going in the wrong direction.

*Praise the Lord for His steadfast love even when we wander
away from Him. Pray He once again will guide you back
to the road leading to His eternal dwelling place.*

KEEP RIGHT

FOLLOW THE NARROW ROAD

DAY 27

Casualties along the Journey

Satan is so much more in earnest than we are—buys up the opportunity while we are wondering how much it will cost.
~Amy Carmichael

Be sober, be vigilant; because your adversary the devil walks about like a roaring lion, seeking whom he may devour.
(1 Peter 5:8)

Abel Tasman's Dutch East India Company expedition encountered the Māori tribes along the journey off the coast of New Zealand. A few days of communication with one local tribe convinced Tasman that a friendly meeting was possible. So, he sent some of his sailors off on a small boat to engage the Māori, but the men faced violence and death instead of a friendly greeting.

Could disembarking European sailors have been seen as an invasion of creatures known as Patupaiarehe by the Māori? In Māori mythology, Patupaiarehe were fair-skinned, supernatural, human-like beings. The reason for the *Māori's* response to the visitors will never be known because Tasman ordered the ships to move on to escape the warriors. More than a century would pass before another meeting between Europeans, and the Māori occurred.

This encounter between the Māori and the sailors in Tasman's expedition illustrates how we often can't possibly determine why we may be under attack. But scripture does offer a solution to the confusing situations we face along our journey. James 4:7 tells us the first requirement—submit to God. Only then do we have the power to do the second thing: resist the devil, who will flee from us.

Praise the Lord for His patience and everlasting love.
Pray that when you are in your darkest days, He will empower you
as you submit to Him and give you strength to resist the devil.

KEEP RIGHT

FOLLOW THE NARROW ROAD

DAY 28

The Rest of Our Journey

*Most of the things we need to be most fully alive
never come in busyness. They grow in rest.*
—Mark Buchanan

Now Jacob's well was there. Jesus therefore, being wearied
from His journey, sat thus by the well. It was about the sixth hour.
(John 4:6)

Each of us must stop and rest at some point. We often don't realize how much we need that rest until after we allow ourselves to take a break in our journey. We're wasting time and won't accomplish as much if we stop—or so we think.

God had appointed a time for an encounter with a woman He was drawing to Himself. We now know her as the woman at the well. What time did He choose for that encounter? When Jesus stopped to rest.

God gave man the Sabbath Day when He created the world. We must take a Sabbath rest each week or have other rest times in our schedule. God will use this time to advance our journey rather than slow it down. It may be too late if we wait until we're sure we need to stop.

Those of us who are often on the road in our line of work find it difficult to set aside time for rest. But if we don't set aside time, the decision to rest is sometimes made for us when our bodies become worn down to the point that we're unable to continue at our current pace. And we may not have another opportunity if we drive ourselves to exhaustion and have an accident or heart attack.

Rather than waiting until it's too late, shouldn't we plan our own Sabbath rest now?

Praise the Lord for His rest—a place completely free from the chaos of this world. Pray that He will teach you to rest in this physical world and, more importantly, to rest in Him.

DAY 29

The Call of Abraham

You are never too old to set another goal or dream a new dream.
~ C. S. Lewis

Now the Lord had said to Abram: "Get out of your country,
from your family and from your father's house, to a land that I will show
you. I will make you a great nation; I will bless you and make
your name great; and you shall be a blessing. I will bless those
who bless you, and I will curse him who curses you; and in you
all the families of the earth shall be blessed." So Abram departed
as the Lord had spoken to him, and Lot went with him. And Abram
was seventy-five years old when he departed from Haran.
(Genesis 12:1–4)

Some of us may think we may be too old for an adventure. But as long as we have breath and are willing to serve Him, God is not done with us. Abraham's call to journey to the new home God had for him came when he was seventy-five. God described the blessings He was planning to bestow on Abraham. "I will make you a great nation; I will bless you and make your name great; and you shall be a blessing . . . And in you all the families of the earth shall be blessed."

At the time the blessing was given, Abraham was still called Abram, which means Exalted Father. Abram may have been somewhat embarrassed by his name since he was childless. But God would bless him in ways he couldn't have imagined. He changed Abram's name to Abraham, which means "Father of Many Nations." Abraham obeyed God and, according to Romans 4:3, ". . . it was accounted to him for righteousness." Abraham's sojourn was a journey of faith, as is ours. Will we be faithful to Him during our journey?

*Praise the Lord of Eternity for being His child, regardless of
how many years have passed during your journey here.
Pray you will always be open to what He has in store
for the next chapter of your life, as impossible as it may seem.*

DAY 30

The Call of Moses

God does not choose people because of their ability,
but because of their availability.
– Brother Andrew

Now therefore, behold, the cry of the children of Israel has come to
Me, and I have also seen the oppression with which the Egyptians
oppress them. Come now, therefore, and I will send you to Pharaoh
that you may bring My people, the children of Israel, out of Egypt.
(Exodus 3:9–10)

Over a thousand years after the time of Abraham, when Moses was
about eighty years old, God sent him to Pharoah to tell him to let His people
go. Moses had fled from Egypt in fear after committing murder many years
before that time. His journey in the wilderness became a relatively uneventful
forty-year period of domestic life in his father-in-law's household.

Perhaps Moses thought God was done with him because of his past failures.
But the greatest call Moses would ever receive came as he performed the
rather mundane task of watching over sheep. The sight of an unconsumed
burning bush changed the trajectory of his life—and forever altered the history
of his people and the world. There, he heard God's voice telling him to
take off his shoes because he stood on holy ground.

Where we are in our journey may be due to events that have led us to
what we think are days spent living a mundane life. But we must be ready
for God's call, for He may use supernatural elements to move us in another
direction at any time. It could come through prayer and prophetic direction.
Or something else. We likely won't know until it happens. Moses had never
seen an unconsumed burning bush, after all.

Praise the Lord for being the Great Deliverer. Pray He will prepare your heart for the call He has for you and your faith will be strengthened, so you have courage to say yes and go when that call comes.

KEEP RIGHT

FOLLOW THE NARROW ROAD

DAY 31

The Call of Bezalel—And Stephen King?

How exactly does God want us to use our talents for Him? Two
ways: blessing others and building His kingdom.
~Dave Ramsey

See, I have called by name Bezalel the son of Uri, the son of Hur, of the
tribe of Judah. And I have filled him with the Spirit of God, in wisdom,
in understanding, in knowledge, and in all manner of workmanship, to
design artistic works, to work in gold, in silver, in bronze, in cutting jewels
for setting, in carving wood, and to work in all manner of workmanship.
(Exodus 31:2–5)

Bezalel lived in the days of Moses, Israel's greatest prophet and leader, but
God no less called Bezalel. He and the other craftsmen were given their skills
for a purpose. God gave Moses a vision of how the tabernacle in the wilderness
was to be built. Bezalel oversaw the work to bring the vision to completion.

Unfortunately, many of us wait for a burning bush or an angel to show
up before we put one foot in front of the other and start walking. Or put it
in gear and go. But the sovereign God of the universe prompted even horror
novelist Stephen King to say in a letter to a young poet, "If God gives you
something you can do, why in God's name wouldn't you do it?"

Moses didn't wait for the burning bush. It appeared when the time was
right. Nor did he wait for an Angel before He came. The Angel appeared
when the time was right.

What has God given us that we seem to do well? He gave us those skills
for a purpose. Let's use our gifts to serve Him in our travels. Why wouldn't we?

Praise the Lord for bestowing upon you the incredible gift of being a part of His Kingdom building. Pray He will provide more opportunities for you to use your skills, wisdom, and knowledge to build His Kingdom wherever your travels take you.

DAY 32

Your Call to Adventure

If the path before you is clear, you're probably on someone else's.
~Joseph Campbell

Do not remember the former things,
Nor consider the things of old.
Behold, I will do a new thing,
Now it shall spring forth;
Shall you not know it?
I will even make a road in the wilderness,
And rivers in the desert.
(Isaiah 43:18–19)

Our journey started when the Lord formed us in our mother's womb. Even then, He had a plan for us (Psalm 139:13–16). The beginning of one leg of our journey has overlapped the last since that time. All the steps we have taken are but stages of one incredible journey. Although he was not a Christian, Joseph Campbell, author of *The Hero with a Thousand Faces,* deeply understood God's creation. He acquired this knowledge by studying the stories and traditions of many different people groups.

The great stories we love follow a pattern Campbell called the Hero's Journey. Every hero's journey will be filled with challenges and numerous high and low points. Transformation comes at the end. Think your journey is boring? Think again. Your journey here has meaning and is a call to adventure!

Every significant character in the Bible starts with this call to adventure. Reading about their lives and the Hero's Journey others experienced can help us better understand our call to adventure.

Praise the Lord for being the fantastic, creative adventurer He is.
You are made in His image, so pray He will give you a vision
of your sojourn here as the call to adventure it is.

DAY 33

All to the Glory of God

When God gives us a talent it is our responsibility
to hone it for His purpose and glory.
~ Yoshiko Sakurai

Therefore, whether you eat or drink, or whatever you do,
do all to the glory of God.
(1 Corinthians 10:31)

Thorvald Asvaldsson was kicked out of Norway for murdering a man, who was said to be just one of many victims of Thorvald's wrath. He settled in Iceland with his son Erik Thorvaldsson. Not to be outdone, Erik was forced to leave Iceland after murdering *two* men. Erik, better known as Erik the Red, discovered Greenland after he was booted out of his homeland.

Erik's son, Leif Erikson, returned to the family's ancestral home of Norway. Instead of killing someone as Dad and Grandad had done, he gave his life to Christ. Leif Erikson was commissioned by King Olaf of Norway to spread the Christian faith and build churches.

Leif Erikson discovered what he called Vinland, which we now know as Newfoundland, about 400 years before Christopher Columbus when his ship was blown off course on the trip back to Greenland. He learned from his father but used his talents to spread the Gospel for the Kingdom.

Whatever our family history, we are new creatures in Christ. We may think God can't use us since we come from dysfunctional families. But is there such a thing as a functional family in this world? Dysfunction seems to be the norm.

So, praise the Lord, sojourner! We know God can turn around any family situation and use it for His glory. And our fellow dysfunctional sojourners need our help.

Praise the Lord for being the Great Deliverer He is! Pray he will break the bonds of your past and your family history, so you may help bring deliverance and a new life to others.

KEEP RIGHT

FOLLOW THE NARROW ROAD

DAY 34

Beam Me Up, Jesus

"Arise and go toward the south"—Philip did not receive
any other instructions because God wanted him,
like He does you and me, to take that first step first.
~Joseph Prince

Now when they came up out of the water, the Spirit of the Lord caught
Philip away, so that the eunuch saw him no more; and he went on his
way rejoicing. But Philip was found at Azotus. And passing through, he
preached in all the cities till he came to Caesarea.
(Acts 8:39–40)

After an angel of the Lord sent Philip to preach to the Ethiopian official,
He swept him away to Azotus. Think the writers of Star Trek came up with
the idea of teleportation? Think again. The Bible is one amazing book. God
teleported Philip away in one of the more unique miracles in Scripture.

How often have we said, "Where did the time go?" We let time slip
away by wasting it with mindless entertainment instead of paying attention
to things of eternal significance.

Philip had no time to waste. He followed God's plan for him, and that
plan was not complicated. An angel of the Lord said, "Arise and go" (Acts
8:26). "So he arose and went" (Acts 8:27). If we want the same results, we
must follow the same pattern: go when He says to go.

Let's not waste another day with useless things during our sojourn here.
Will he teleport us when we follow His call? Possibly. We know for sure that
if we belong to Him, we'll travel up to meet Him in the air when the trumpet
of God sounds (1 Thessalonians 4:16–17).

Praise the Lord for everything He has taught you, even during "wasted" times. Pray for wisdom in knowing which activities are time wasters and useless to the Kingdom.

KEEP RIGHT

FOLLOW THE NARROW ROAD

DAY 35

Coming Down from the Mountaintop

The Lord meets us in the valley with food and drink. We are often unaware of this until we get past the crisis and we look back to see God's hand of care and protection. Having been through the dark valley ourselves, we may offer the Lord's comfort to those who are walking in the dark valleys now.
~Frank Viola

But Peter and those with him were heavy with sleep; and when they were fully awake, they saw His glory and the two men who stood with Him. Then it happened, as they were parting from Him, that Peter said to Jesus, "Master, it is good for us to be here; and let us make three tabernacles: one for You, one for Moses, and one for Elijah."—not knowing what he said.
(Luke 9:32–33)

The disciples witnessed Jesus' transfiguration along with that of Moses and Elijah when He brought them up onto a mountain to pray. Peter sought to set up tabernacles or tents for them so they could stay. Jesus taught his disciples spiritual experiences are good in themselves, but those experiences serve a greater purpose. We receive fuel for our mission when we reach those spiritual heights. When we come back down, we may travel through dark valleys. Our experiences, whether high or low, are used to minister to others.

Have you ever had a profound spiritual experience during a church service or retreat? That time will never be forgotten. You may never reach such heights again—or maybe you will! We seek God's presence daily, but we know our experiences with Him during our sojourn here may include visits to the depths of a dark valley along with those joyous trips to the mountaintop.

The remembrance of mountaintop experiences can be a source of encouragement to help keep us focused on the work ahead when it seems we are trudging through harsh terrain in the valley. His ways are higher than our ways (Isaiah 55:8–9). We won't always understand the reason for every stop along our journey.

Praise the Lord for His presence on the mountaintop and in the valley. Pray He will work in you on the mountaintop and in the valley to spiritually strengthen you for whatever you may face during your journey.

KEEP RIGHT

FOLLOW THE NARROW ROAD

DAY 36

Carrying Our Cross on the Journey

*Naturally, men are prone to spin themselves a web of opinions out of
their own brain and to have a religion that may be called their own.
They are far readier to make themselves a faith than to receive
that which God hath formed to their hands; are far readier
to receive a doctrine that tends to their carnal commodity,
or honor, or delight, than one that tends to self-denial.*
~ Richard Baxter

Then He said to them all, "If anyone desires to come after Me,
let him deny himself, and take up his cross daily, and follow Me.
For whoever desires to save his life will lose it,
but whoever loses his life for My sake will save it."
(Luke 9:23–24)

Jesus calls us to travel light, but the one thing we must carry is our cross. When Jesus picked up His cross, He took it to His death. To follow Jesus means to live as He lived. When he tells us to do the same, He is speaking figuratively. We must die to ourselves and for our sins.

The opposite of carrying our cross daily is to be one who 'desires to save his life' but loses it in the process. Saving your life in this sense would be preserving the way you lived apart from Christ—loving what the world loves and going after the world's idols. But that was never true life. To find true life and freedom in Christ requires you to trade your sinful life for His righteousness. Jesus called it 'losing his life for My sake.'

What part of our old life apart from Christ do we know He would have us give up, so we may follow Him more faithfully? Is there anything in our lives that are off-limits to Him? We may have to let Him dig deep here. Are we holding on to past hurts and refusing to forgive another? Or holding on to deeply ingrained behaviors that harm only ourselves?

Let's not allow those things to hinder our journey in the future.

Praise the Lord for carrying His cross to His death, so we may have life. Pray He will give you the courage to drop all the burdens hindering your journey so you may have the strength to carry your cross with conviction.

DAY 37

Long Road Home

*We foolish mortals sometimes live through years
not realizing how short life is and that TODAY is your life.*
~Edith Schaeffer

But, beloved, do not forget this one thing, that with the Lord one day is
as a thousand years, and a thousand years as one day.
(2 Peter 3:8)

In 1271, Marco Polo left Venice for a fantastic adventure with his father Niccolo, and Uncle Maffeo. Marco met the powerful Mongol ruler Kublai Kahn for the first time at the end of their journey to the Mongol Empire. He was just seventeen years old when he left home.

The elder Polos met the Kahn during an earlier visit. The Kahn was so inspired by their Christian faith that he asked them to return with 100 teachers so his people could learn about the Christ of whom they spoke. But only two priests departed with the Polos on that second journey. Can you imagine how different our world would be if 100 teachers had made the trip back? Sadly, even the two priests who agreed to accompany them turned back, unwilling to endure the harsh conditions.

The Kahn admired Marco Polo and provided him unlimited access to his domain. Marco returned home to Venice about twenty-four years after his journey began, but his adventure wasn't over. Shortly after his return, Marco Polo was captured in battle and thrown in prison, where he met an adventure writer. This meeting is why we know of his journey today.

When our journey seems the longest, it can become difficult for us to focus on the narrow road ahead, and we may begin to lose sight of our destination. But we only have one day in which we have control of our journey. That day is today. Let's say yes to His call and go.

Praise the Lord for giving you life TODAY. Pray He will provide you
with an eternal perspective and strength for your journey,
especially when the road seems long and hard.

DAY 38

The Old Paths

The heart of man is the same in every age.
The spiritual medicine which it requires is always the same.
-*J. C. Ryle*

Thus says the Lord: "Stand in the ways and see, and ask for the old
paths, where the good way is, and walk in it; then you will find rest for
your souls. But they said, 'We will not walk in it.'
(Jeremiah 6:16)

When the Interstate Highway System's roads spread out across the
American landscape like great concrete ribbons, travel times shortened con-
siderably. Giant trucks rumbling down those new roads became the lifeblood
of the nation. The old roads soon became relics of days gone by.

Route 66, the 'The Mother Road' of *The Grapes of Wrath* fame, is perhaps
the best example. Once glorified in song and literature, this road to adventure is now a shell of its former self. Largely abandoned in many places, its
role now, rather than having any practical function, seems to be to provide a
place for nostalgia where people may slow down and see the landmarks and
historic sites that commemorate bygone days.

The 'old paths' Jeremiah refers to are the ways of the people of God who
feared and loved Him. By the time of the days in which the prophet lived
and wrote, most of God's people refused to follow Him. The old paths were
left behind and fell into disrepair.

Times have changed, but God has not changed. And human nature has
not changed. Just as no new paths to enlightenment or spiritual fulfillment
existed then, none exist now outside of Jesus. This should comfort us. The
New Covenant is the fulfillment of the Old. Jesus Christ is the same yester-
day, today, and forever (Hebrews 13:8).

Praise the Lord for His unchanging nature. Pray He will help you return to the old ways, which are new every day and everlasting.

DAY 39

Walk Circumspectly

To call yourself a child of God is one thing. To be called a child of God
by those who watch your life is another thing altogether.
~Max Lucado

See then that you walk circumspectly, not as fools but as wise,
redeeming the time, because the days are evil. Therefore do not be
unwise, but understand what the will of the Lord is.
(Ephesians 5:15–17)

We know that to walk circumspectly is to walk wisely and carefully. But so many of us have walked otherwise, which we know is the opposite of wise. The foolish mistakes we made in the past may hinder our journey even today. In Ephesians, Peter was writing to people just like us. He said we should walk circumspectly because 'the days are evil.'

We often say we live in a fallen world. But fallen into or from what? Has the world not fallen away from the light and into darkness or evil? We know our sojourn here is through a dark and evil world, just like Peter spoke of in his time. How much more difficult it is for us to travel in the dark!

We wouldn't drive down the highway at night without our lights on. And we can't expect to be able to stay on God's highway without allowing Him to direct us so we may 'understand what the will of the Lord is.'

Let's turn on those lights. Redeeming time could mean we get back lost time. How? By repenting of our foolishness and allowing God to use those 'wasted' years to help mold us into the men or women of God we are meant to be. Rather than hindering our journey now, those foolish mistakes we made in the past may help us have compassion for the lost and hurting souls we encounter during our travels in these evil days in which we live.

*Praise the Lord for being the redeemer He is! Pray He will help you
be obedient to His will as you take each step forward on your journey
(Psalm 37:23).*

DAY 40

To Die Is Gain

Some day you will read in the papers that D. L. Moody, of East
Northfield, is dead. Don't you believe a word of it!
At that moment I shall be more alive than I am now.
~Dwight L. Moody

For to me, to live is Christ, and to die is gain.
But if I live on in the flesh, this will mean fruit from my labor;
yet what I shall choose I cannot tell.
(Philippians 1:21–22)

At this point in Paul's life, it seemed to be an eternity from the time he was known as Saul of Tarsus and had the garments of those who stoned Stephen laid at his feet. And in a sense, it was. Those who murdered the martyr took off their outer garments to better their aim and perhaps protect themselves from the spatter of blood. But Saul had Stephen's blood on his hands, and he knew it.

Of course, we now know this man as the great Apostle Paul. Books attributed to Paul comprise about half of the books in the New Testament. Paul stepped into Eternity when he met the Lord he had persecuted. Jesus embraced Him with open arms.

At this point, he had received forty lashes minus one five times (the one was held back because people believed forty lashes would kill a man), had been beaten with rods three times, and three times was shipwrecked. Like Stephen, he was stoned once, but unlike Stephen, he lived. Paul wrote his letter to the Philippians from prison. His attitude? If he lived, he reasoned, Christ would be magnified by the fruit of his labor. If he died, it would be gain for him.

Keep going, fellow sojourner. Your journey here has meaning. If our paths don't cross on this side, we'll meet on the other.

Praise the Lord for placing Eternity in your heart. Pray He will give you a heart filled with love for Heaven and His presence more and more with each passing day until your journey Home comes to an end.

THE
SOJOURNER'S
Road Home

KEEP RIGHT

FOLLOW THE NARROW ROAD

STAY ON THE ROAD

I am not troubled by the things in the Bible which I do not
understand, but I am troubled by those things which I do understand
and which I find very difficult to measure up to.
~Mark Twain

As each one has received a gift, minister it to one another, as good
stewards of the manifold grace of God. If anyone speaks, let him
speak as the oracles of God. If anyone ministers, let him do it as with
the ability which God supplies, that in all things God may be glorified
through Jesus Christ, to whom belong the glory and the dominion
forever and ever. Amen.
(1 Peter 4:10–11)

We may not know how many more days our Lord has for us in our sojourn through this fallen world, but as long as we're here, we are missionaries for God during our travels. Charles Spurgeon said every Christian is either a missionary or an imposter.

We all have different gifts and talents and will likely never be the great preacher Spurgeon was. But God has not called most of us to preach—at least not from a pulpit. Spurgeon also said, ". . . the world does not read the Bible; the world reads Christians! "You are the light of the world . . ." (Matthew 5:14).

We may be the closest things to a Bible our fellow sojourners have ever read, so let's make sure our actions and words lift up our Maker. Our feelings of inadequacy because of past failures often keep us from moving forward. But God would not have us stay silent about the Good News! (Matthew 5:16).

To paraphrase the great Yogi Berra, it ain't over until your sojourn ends. Since you're reading this, God is not done with you, so there's still work for you. We are all works in progress. Let's not worry about making mistakes. Our fellow sojourners need our help now. We'll borrow Ruth Bell Graham's words for our gravestones:

End of Construction. Thank you for your patience.

JOURNEY'S END?

God looks forward to rewarding us with the completion of our salvation.
~ Dr. Vergil Schmidt

And the nations of those who are saved shall walk in its light, and the
kings of the earth bring their glory and honor into it. Its gates shall not
be shut at all by day (there shall be no night there). And they shall
bring the glory and the honor of the nations into it.
(Rev 21:24–26)

Christopher Columbus landed in the Americas in 1492. It was an unplanned stop in what was meant to be a passage around the globe. He stumbled upon a New World in which he explored and established settlements. It turned out to be the first of four voyages in search of a direct route by sea between Europe and the enormous trading markets of Asia.

Columbus died not knowing he discovered continents unknown to anyone in the Old World. But even death couldn't stop the travels of this great explorer. His body continued to sail those routes as his remains were moved from the Old World to the New and back again before those remains were finally laid to rest in Spain over 400 years after his first voyage.

87

Where will we travel after our death in Christ? We know our journey leads to God in the spiritual realm. A new heaven and a new earth will descend one day. Kings will worship there. So shall we.

What will eternity be like for us? Will we continue to travel? That seems likely since He's given us a heart for travel here. We know our journey has just begun and it is beyond our capabilities to imagine what He has in store for us (1 Corinthians 2:9).

THE ROAD AHEAD

You have taken a big step in your spiritual journey by completing The Sojourner's Road Home. What next? Let's explore some ideas that may help you during the rest of your sojourn here.

Take Time for Praise and Prayer Each Day

Whatever your schedule, set aside regular time for praise and prayer as part of your spiritual practice. Remember Day 13: The Pilgrim's Pathway? Christian's journey is recorded in *The Pilgrim's Progress* by John Bunyan. Reflect on each day of your journey thus far and how it may help to guide you going forward. Sojourner is a synonym for the word pilgrim. Continue to record your own progress, pilgrim.

Seek Out Community

Connect with other sojourners for times of fellowship, Bible study, or prayer, and share your thoughts about your personal journey. Relationships with your fellow sojourners will provide support when times are tough and will be a source of joy when you share your victories and rejoice in theirs. You can visit TheSojournersRoadHome to find groups to help connect you with like-minded sojourners.

Find Another Sojourner to Partner with You on Your Journey

Reach out to a fellow sojourner through one of the resources at TheSojournersRoadHome so they may walk with you as you seek direction and encouragement along the way in your journey. There are far more like-minded people out there than you may realize who will be glad to partner with you once you take that first step.

Put Your Faith into Action

Remember Day 15: Support Your Fellow Sojourners? Your fellow sojourners need your help as much as you need theirs. All who have chosen to travel the narrow road are part of one Body (1 Corinthians 12:12–27). The Sojourner's Road Home is about returning to the heart of God. Do something every day that will bring glory and honor to God—like helping someone in need, especially those who can't repay you (Matthew 25:35–40). Or share an inspiring, uplifting message for other sojourners who may be struggling with their own spiritual journey. There will always be something you can do each day as you continue your journey.

Share Your Experience on Your 40-Day Journey at TheSojournersRoadHome.com

ABOUT JIM WOODFORD

J im Woodford was born in the Canadian province of Newfoundland. His father died when he was just two years of age. Jim was raised in the home of his maternal grandparents, where he developed a fascination with aircraft at an early age since there was a seaplane dock at the edge of the river where the family lived.

That fascination led to a lifelong love of flying. His career as a pilot began when he was nineteen years old, making him one of the youngest licensed pilots in Canada. Jim would fly small aircraft to lakes in remote regions of the country as other means of transport were often unavailable, especially during the bone-chilling Canadian winters.

His career path elevated him into the cockpits of ever larger aircraft until he became captain of a major airline. Jim traveled extensively during his tenure as a pilot. His travels have taken him from Toronto in his native Canada to Timbuktu and everywhere in between.

But an unplanned destination forever changed the course of Jim's life. A flight to Heaven caused him to return home a changed man. He has since dedicated his life to helping take as many passengers with him as he can on his return flight. His mission also includes encouraging believers to dedicate their lives to the Savior he met on the journey to his ultimate home. You may learn more about Jim Woodford and his ministry by reading *Heaven, An Unexpected Journey,* and by visiting his website.

Jim's love for flying is matched only by his passion for horses. He now resides in New Brunswick, Canada, with his wife Lorraine and his beloved horses.

ABOUT THE AUTHOR

Kelly Mack McCoy chose to pursue a life-long dream of becoming an author after a life-altering event changed the trajectory of his life. John Floyd Mills, a writer with the San Antonio Light newspaper, approached him about co-authoring a series of novels about a trucker-turned-pastor-turned-trucker who hits the road again after his wife's murder. But the two never wrote the books. John went on to write two novels alone while Kelly Mack McCoy took up the trucker-turned-pastor-turned-trucker project on his own.

However, it would take another life-changing event to motivate him to see the project through to completion. That event was the death of John Floyd Mills. The first completed project would become the highly acclaimed novel *Rough Way to the High Way*. You hold the second completed project in your hands now. Thank you.

In *The Sojourner's Road Home*, Kelly Mack McCoy draws from life lessons learned during his forty-plus years on the road. For thirty-five of those years, he has been a Christian, so he is keenly aware of how time away from home and other Christians can affect our spiritual and emotional health.

Besides the sense of isolation and sometimes even despair experienced by those who spend much of their time on the road, their travels often come with the high cost of damaged relationships and even physical illnesses. During his challenging travels on the road of life, the author learned how steadfastly holding onto your faith during these times can have a powerful effect on your spiritual life and state of mind.

If you would like to see more from this author, please leave a review.

A free ebook edition is available with the purchase of this book.

To claim your free ebook edition:

1. Visit MorganJamesBOGO.com
2. Sign your name CLEARLY in the space
3. Complete the form and submit a photo of the entire copyright page
4. You or your friend can download the ebook to your preferred device

Morgan James BOGO™

A **FREE** ebook edition is available for you or a friend with the purchase of this print book.

CLEARLY SIGN YOUR NAME ABOVE

Instructions to claim your free ebook edition:
1. Visit MorganJamesBOGO.com
2. Sign your name CLEARLY in the space above
3. Complete the form and submit a photo of this entire page
4. You or your friend can download the ebook to your preferred device

Print & Digital Together Forever.

Snap a photo   Free ebook   Read anywhere

Printed in the USA
CPSIA information can be obtained
at www.ICGtesting.com
JSHW021458110823
46405JS00001B/17